# Zoom in on
# EDUCATIONAL ROBOTS

**Sara L. Latta**

E Enslow Publishing
101 W. 23rd Street
Suite 240
New York, NY 10011
USA

enslow.com

# WORDS TO KNOW

**ecosystem**  Everything that exists in a given environment, including living and nonliving things.

**microphone**  A device into which people speak or sing in order to transmit the sounds of their voices.

**program**  To give a set of instructions to a machine. A program can also mean the set of instructions itself.

**robot**  A machine that can carry out a series of actions by itself.

**sensor**  A part that detects light, temperature, pressure, sound, or motion.

# CONTENTS

Students learn math skills as they figure out how to program a robot.

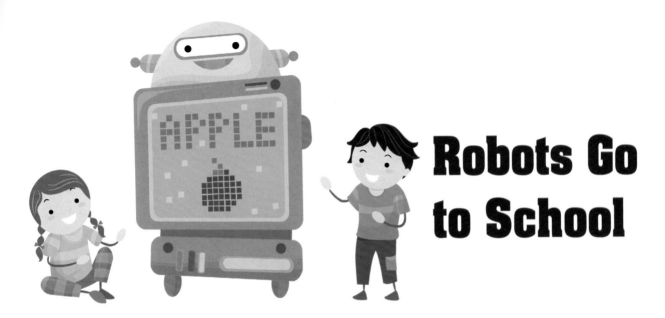

# Robots Go to School

Your classroom has tools to help you learn. There are books to read. You sit at a desk. You write with pencils and paper. Some classrooms have new tools to help students learn. They have robots.

## What Are Robots?

Robots are machines. They can carry out jobs by themselves. Computers control most robots. The computers tell the robots

These educational robots have hands that can grip. They can also recognize faces and dance!

what to do. Robots have parts that allow them to move, grab, turn, or lift. They have sensors like cameras or microphones. Sensors tell the robots about people or things nearby. This information helps robots figure out the best way to do their job.

> ### What's in a Name?
> The word "robot" comes from a Czech word. It means "forced work."

## What Are Educational Robots Like?

Robots come in many shapes and sizes. They may look like people made of plastic or metal. They may smile or laugh. Others are machines with a screen that shows the face of a real person controlling the robot. A ball-shaped robot teaches kids how to program a computer. Robots can fly, roll, or crawl.

## Why Don't All Classrooms Have Robots?

Robots can cost a lot of money. But they are getting cheaper all the time. Teachers like them because they help students learn. Soon there will be robots in more classrooms.

**Some classrooms have robots. You can see the face of the student controlling this classroom robot on the screen.**

# Long-Distance Robots

Robots can help kids who are too sick to go to school. A robot goes to school instead of the student. The student controls the robot from home. The robot is mounted on wheels. It has a video camera and a microphone. The robot lets the student see and hear what's going on in the classroom.

The teachers and classmates can see the student on a screen. A microphone lets their voice be heard. The student at home can see and talk to the teacher and other kids at school.

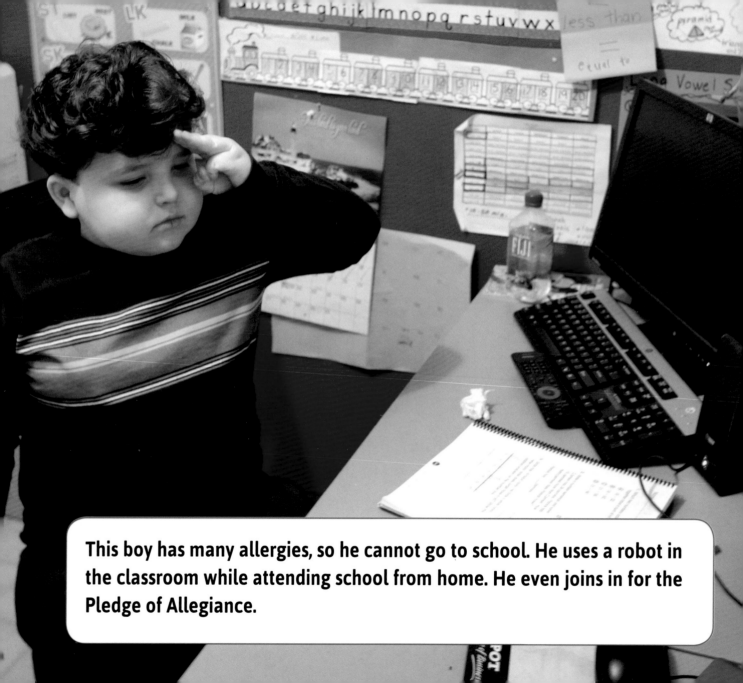

This boy has many allergies, so he cannot go to school. He uses a robot in the classroom while attending school from home. He even joins in for the Pledge of Allegiance.

## Teacher Robots

Robots will never take the place of teachers. But robots can help teachers do their jobs better. Some schools in South Korea

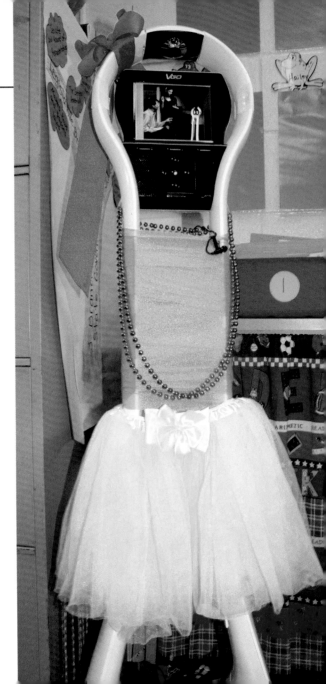

### Pick Me!

The Vgo robot takes a student's place at school. It lets students raise their hands by flashing its headlights. Some kids like to dress their robots. One at-home student put her robot (*right*) in a pink tutu, a bow, and beads.

Students wave hello to a friend who uses a robot to attend classes.

do not have enough English teachers. They use a robot called Engkey instead. An English teacher many miles from the classroom controls Engkey. The students can see the teacher's face on Engkey's screen. The teacher can see the students through a video camera. The teacher and students talk together through the robot's microphone and speakers.

Other teaching robots can mark students as present or absent. A robot dog teaches students dance moves.

# Robots for Students with Special Needs

Our brains help us understand the things we see and hear. Some children have brains that makes it hard for them to understand those signals. They struggle to understand what feelings look like on people's faces. Talking to people can be confusing.

Children with these problems sometimes find it easier to talk to robots. Robots can look a little like humans, but it is easier to understand the looks on their "faces." A small

Nao helps this boy learn everyday skills.

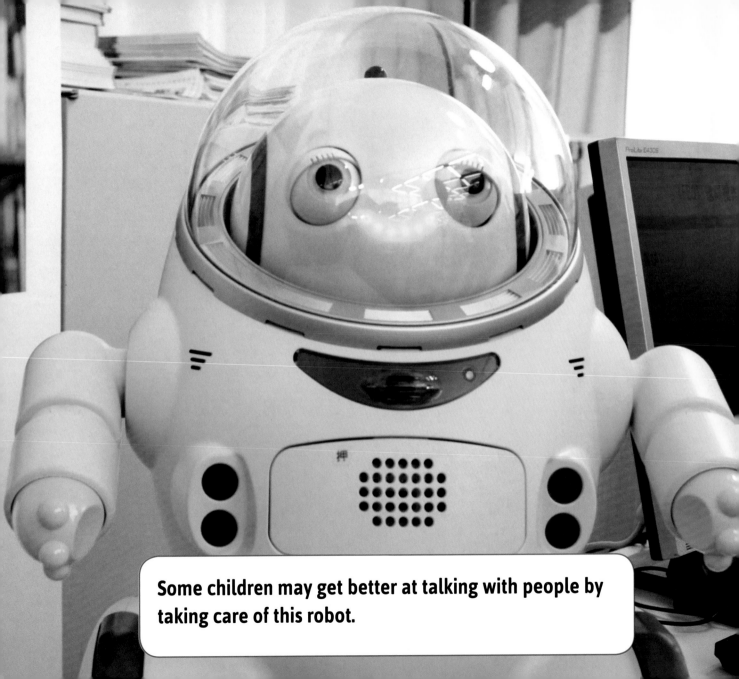

Some children may get better at talking with people by taking care of this robot.

classroom robot called Nao can dance, sing, and clap. Nao helps children learn what happy or sad looks like. Playing games with Nao helps them build the skills they need to understand people.

## Do Robots Have Feelings?

Robots can be programmed to laugh or cry. They can tell when people are happy or sad. But they do not have any feelings.

# Learning About Robots

Building and programming robots is not just for adults. Kids can make robots from everyday things around the house or classroom. There are special LEGO kits for making robots. It is fun to build machines!

Even children in kindergarten can learn to program robots. A program tells the robot how to carry out actions or tasks. Learning how to program robots teaches kids a certain kind of thinking. They learn new ways of working through a problem.

You can build a robot with LEGO kits.

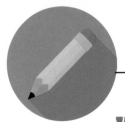
## Kids Teaching Robots

Robots can teach children. But kids can also teach robots! Has your teacher ever asked you to help a friend solve a math problem? Has a classmate helped you with spelling? Teachers know that students learn a subject better when they help another student learn.

Some students are teaching robots subjects like earth science or history. Unlike humans, robots don't feel embarrassed when they get something wrong. It is fun to see how robots learn. A student teaching a robot called

### Robot Contests

Many schools have robot contests. Teams of students compete to build and program the best robots.

Betty's Brain might want to teach it about ecosystems. The student teacher tells Betty's Brain the words for things in an ecosystem: frog, river, bird. The student helps Betty's Brain link them together. And the robot helps the student practice checking his or her facts.

The Dash robot teaches students how to program a computer.

# ACTIVITY:
## PROGRAM A ROBOT

Robots need good computer programs to tell them what to do. They can't make any decisions on their own. In this activity, one person will be the computer programmer. The other will be the "robot." Any other people will be the judges. They let the programmer and robot know if they are not following the rules.

1. Pick a task for the robot to carry out. Use your imagination! For example, the programmer might choose to have the robot write a message on a whiteboard.

2. The programmer gives commands for the robot to follow. Remember, the commands must be very specific! For example, you need to tell the robot exactly how to get to the whiteboard. What direction should it face? How many steps does it need to take? Where is the marker? How can it recognize the marker? How does it pick it up? How does it write? The list goes on and on.

3. Here are some good examples of programming commands:
   - Move forward five steps.
   - Find the marker.
   - Grasp the marker between your thumb and pointer finger.
   - Lift the marker to shoulder height and place it on the whiteboard.
   - Write the letter X.

4. Here are some examples of bad commands:
   - Walk to the whiteboard.
   - Find something to write with.
   - Write a sentence on the whiteboard.
   - Write whatever you like.

5. If the programmer or the robot breaks the rules, the judges let them know!

# LEARN MORE

## Books

Schulman, Mark. *TIME for Kids Explorers: Robots*. New York, NY: TIME for Kids, 2014.

Stewart, Melissa. *National Geographic Readers: Robots*. Washington, DC: National Geographic Children's Books, 2014.

Tuchman, Gail. *Robots*. New York, NY: Scholastic, 2015.

## Websites

**Robotics: Facts**
*idahoptv.org/sciencetrek/topics/robots/facts.cfm*
Check out many interesting facts about robots.

**Robots for Kids**
*sciencekids.co.nz/robots.html*
Learn more about the world of robots with games, facts, projects, quizzes, and videos.

# INDEX

Published in 2018 by Enslow Publishing, LLC.
101 W. 23rd Street, Suite 240, New York, NY 10011

Cataloging-in-Publication Data
Names: Latta, Sara L.
Title: Zoom in on educational robots / Sara L. Latta.
Description: New York : Enslow Publishing, 2018 | Series: Zoom in on robots | Includes bibliographical references and index. | Audience: Grades K to 3.
 Identifiers: ISBN 9780766092273 (library bound) | ISBN 9780766094468 (pbk.) | ISBN 9780766094475 (6 pack)
Subjects: LCSH: Robots—Juvenile literature. | Robotics—Juvenile literature. | Educational technology—Juvenile literature.
Classification: LCC TJ211.2 L375 2018 | DDC 629.8/92—dc23

Printed in the United States of America

**To Our Readers:** We have done our best to make sure all website addresses in this book were active and appropriate when we went to press. However, the author and the publisher have no control over and assume no liability for the material available on those websites or on any websites they may link to. Any comments or suggestions can be sent by email to customerservice@enslow.com.

**Photo Credits:** Cover, p. 1 SpeedKingz/Shutterstock.com; p. 4 Westend61/Getty Images; p. 6 Ethan Miller/Getty Images; p. 8 BSIP/UIG/Getty Images; pp. 10, 11, 16, 21 © AP Images; p. 12 Portland Press Herald/Getty Images; p. 15 Photodiem/Shutterstock.com; p. 19 AlesiaKan/Shutterstock.com; p. 22 Monkey Business Images/Shutterstock.com; graphic elements cover, p. 1 (background) Perzeus/Shutterstock.com; pp. 2, 3, 22, 23 kotoffei/Shutterstock.com; pp. 5, 9, 13, 18 Lorelyn Medina/Shutterstock.com; pp. 8, 20 Artem Twin/Shutterstock.com.